USBORNE GUIDE TO COMPL JARGON

ILLUSTRATED

Corinne Stockley and Lisa Watts
Technical consultant: Andrew Wallis

Designed by Graham Round

Illustrated by Graham Round, Mark Longworth, Martin Newton, Chris Lyon, Graham Smith and Ian Stephen.

Contents

About this book

For most people the words used to describe computers are a whole new language. You need a dictionary to read a computer magazine or book, or even an advertisement for a new computer. This book is a guide to the words a beginner needs to know in order to read or talk about computers. For each word there is a written definition and many of the words are illustrated as well. The words have been specially chosen for people using a home computer, or microcomputer, and there are also a few more advanced words to start you off on more specialized reading.

What is computer jargon?

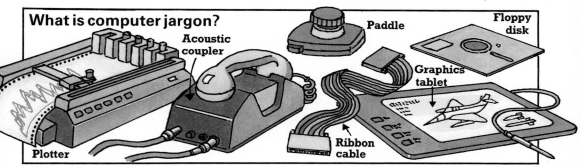

Acoustic coupler

Paddle

Floppy disk

Graphics tablet

Ribbon cable

Plotter

All specialized subjects have their own jargon so that experts can talk and write about them. For instance, mathematicians have maths words, musicians need musical terms and engineers have their own technical terms. Computers are such a new technological development that lots of new words have had to be invented to describe things which never existed before. The words have come from lots of different sources. There are words from our normal language which have been given new twists of meaning, technical terms, manufacturer's trade names, abbreviations made into words and slang words. There's even a jargon word for all these words – buzzwords!

New words are being invented all the time, so no book of computer jargon can be entirely up to date. This book, though, gives you all the words you need to gain a basic understanding of computers and you will soon find that learning about them is not as difficult as the jargon makes it seem.

How to use this book

The words in this book are arranged thematically, that is, by subject. For example, all the words to do with programs are listed together, and so are the graphics words, memory words and words to describe the parts inside a computer. The main subjects are given in the contents list on the opposite page.

To find the explanation for a word you do not understand, look it up in the Wordfinder at the back of the book. The main explanation of the word is given on the page number printed in bold type, **like this**. Other page numbers are places where you can find out more about the word. In the text, words which you may not understand are printed in bold type to show that they are explained in the book and you can look them up in the Wordfinder.

First computer words

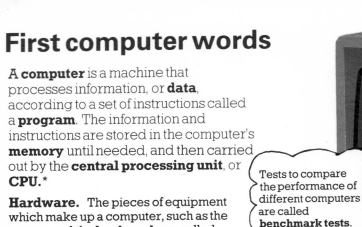

A **computer** is a machine that processes information, or **data**, according to a set of instructions called a **program**. The information and instructions are stored in the computer's **memory** until needed, and then carried out by the **central processing unit**, or **CPU**.*

Tests to compare the performance of different computers are called **benchmark tests**.

Hardware. The pieces of equipment which make up a computer, such as the **screen** and the **keyboard**, are called **hardware**.

Software. All the programs which tell the computer what to do are called **software**. This includes the programs built into the computer when it is made as well as the programs you give it.

Input and **output.** The information which you give a computer is called **input**, and any information it gives you is **output**.

Keyboard. This is where you type information and instructions into the computer. It looks like a typewriter keyboard, but usually has extra keys for giving the computer special instructions.

Keyboard

Keys

Types of computer

Microcomputer. The picture above shows a **microcomputer**, or **micro**. Most micros have built-in keyboards, and are used for many different purposes – in small businesses and schools as well as by home users. They are also called **personal computers** or **home computers**.

Mainframe. This is a very large, powerful computer which is able to process a great deal of information and do lots of jobs at once. Together with all its extra pieces of equipment, it can easily take up a number of rooms. Mainframes are used to keep track of such things as driving licences, phone bills and income tax.

Minicomputer. This is smaller than a **mainframe**. It can deal with a number of things at once, though not as many as a mainframe.

Pocket computer. This is a **microcomputer** small enough to fit into a pocket. Pocket computers run on batteries and usually have a built-in screen.

Games computer. This type of computer is only used for playing games. It cannot usually be programmed to carry out other tasks.

4

*For more about **programs**, see page 32; **memory**, page 10; the **CPU**, page 16.

Screen. This is where the computer displays information. It may be an ordinary television set, or a special screen called a **monitor**. Some computers have their own built-in screen.

Screen

Program

A computer in the process of carrying out a program is said to be **up and running**.

Two computers are **compatible** if programs or equipment meant for one can be used by the other.

Lead connecting computer to TV.

Ports. These are also called **I/O ports** or **input/output ports.** They are sockets in the computer where leads from other equipment are plugged in.

Sockets or ports

Cassettes

Cassette recorder

Peripheral. Any extra piece of equipment which you can connect to a computer is called a **peripheral.** For example, you can use a **cassette recorder** or a **disk drive** to store programs and information on cassettes or disks. Other examples of peripherals are a **printer**, for printing programs or information on paper, and a **plotter** for printing pictures.

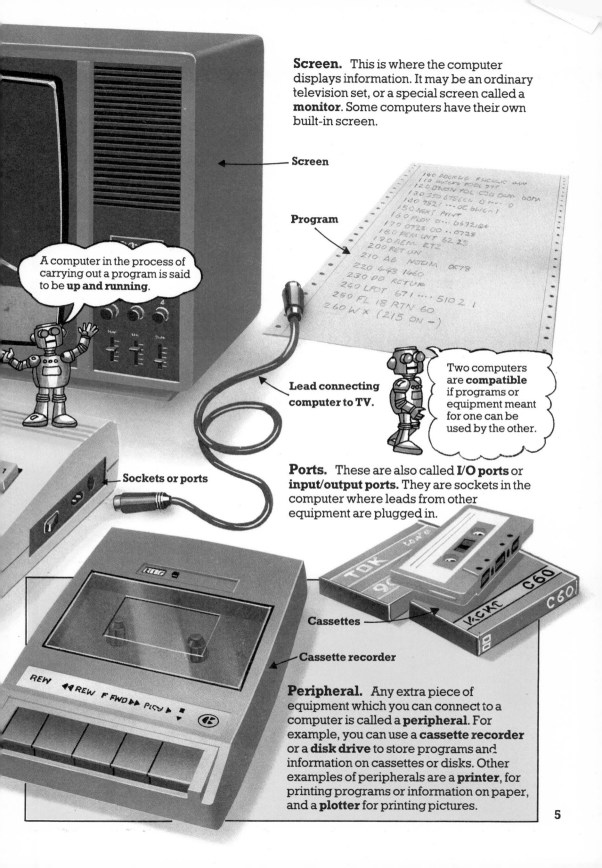

5

Keyboard words

The most common type of computer **keyboard** has keys arranged like a typewriter. It is called a **QWERTY keyboard** after the first six keys of the top row of letters. Most keyboards are **alphanumeric**, which means they have both letter and number keys. Some have a **numeric keypad**, a section with only number keys, and some have keys with **keyword** commands on them. **Keywords** are words in a **programming language** (see page 30) which tell the computer to carry out a particular task, and you need press these keys only once to give the computer the whole word. This is called **one-touch entry** or **single key entry**.

There are several different styles of keyboard. A **touch-sensitive** one is flat, with the keys printed on a special sheet which is sensitive to your touch. A **calculator-style** keyboard has small, springy keys.

Most keyboards have moving keys, spaced and sloped, or **pitched**, as on a typewriter. **Key travel** refers to the distance the keys can go down, and **full travel** means they can be pressed right down. Some keyboards have **auto-repeat**, so that you can repeat a letter by holding the key down. Others have a **repeat key** to press with the key you want to repeat.

Upper case letters are capitals, **lower case** are small letters.

Microcomputer with QWERTY keyboard.

SHIFT key. A key usually has two or more letters or symbols on it. You press SHIFT at the same time as a key to get the top character on the key. The **SHIFT LOCK** key holds the SHIFT key in place. **CAPS LOCK** is another kind of SHIFT key which lets you make capital letters.

Sockets and switches

ON/OFF. For power to the computer.

Analogue* (analog) port or **control port.** For plugging in extra equipment, such as a **joystick** or **light pen.**

Printer port. For plugging in a **printer.**

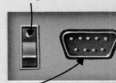

Other keys

Here are some of the special keys on a computer keyboard. Some of them have different names on different computers.

| STOP | BREAK | ESCAPE |

These stop a computer in the middle of running a program.

| RETURN | NEWLINE | ENTER |

You press these at the end of each instruction to tell the computer to carry it out or store it in its memory.

CTRL ◄ This stands for control key. When you press CTRL with another key the computer understands a **control character**. This tells it to carry out a task such as sending information to a printer.

CLR HOME This moves the **cursor** to the top left-hand corner of the screen. When pressed with the **SHIFT key**, it also clears the screen.

ESC ◄ This is a type of control key which you use with other keys to give them different functions.

*For more about **analogue**, see page 20.

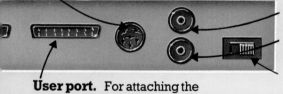

Character set. This is the set of **characters** that a computer can produce. The **ASCII** (American Standard Code for Information Interchange) character set, pronounced "ass-key", is the one used by most microcomputers. It includes all the letters of the alphabet, the digits 0 to 9 and a number of special symbols.

A **character** is any letter, number or symbol.

Function keys. These are also called **user-programmable keys**. You can program the computer to carry out certain tasks whenever you hit a function key, such as printing a word like PRINT or INPUT, which you will need a lot when writing a program. On the ZX81, the function key acts like another **SHIFT key**.

Cursor control keys. These move the **cursor** up, down, left or right. The cursor is the symbol which shows where the next character will appear on the screen.

:e bar. This is for
ng spaces between words.

Cassette port. For attaching a **cassette recorder**. This is sometimes two separate sockets, one for receiving signals from the recorder (**EAR**) and one for sending them to it (**MIC**).

Video port. For the lead to a special kind of screen called a **monitor** (see page 8).

UHF port. For the lead to a television. UHF stands for ultra-high frequency, the type of signals which a TV uses.*

User port. For attaching the computer to other devices you want to control, e.g. a model railway or robot.

Reset. To stop the running of a program or regain control over the computer if it **crashes** (see page 32).

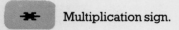 Multiplication sign.

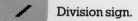 Division sign.

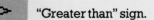 "Greater than" sign.

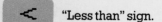 "Less than" sign.

The **dollar** or **string** sign. Used for certain types of **variables** (see page 33).

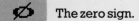 The zero sign.

▲ All these mean "raised to the power of".

The **hash** sign. This is used to indicate **hex** numbers,** e.g. #6.

The **ampersand**. Used to mean "and" or to indicate **hex** numbers.**

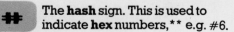

▲ These are symbols from the **ASCII character set**. Most of them do not have any special meaning, but you can print them on the screen just like any other character.

7

*This is the **VHF** (very high frequency) **port** in the USA.

For more about **hex, see page 42.

Screen words

Everything you type into a computer, and all the results it gives you, can be displayed on a **screen**, sometimes called a **VDU (visual display unit)** or **CRT** (see below). It can be an ordinary television or a **monitor**, which looks like a TV, but cannot receive programmes broadcast by television stations.

Cursor. This is a symbol on the screen which shows where the next **character** will be printed. Depending on the computer, it may be a flashing square, an arrowhead, a K or a short line.

Prompt. This is a symbol which appears on the screen when the computer wants information from you. On most computers it is a question mark.

Scroll. When the screen is full of text most computers automatically move all the lines up to make space at the bottom and lose a line at the top. This is called **scrolling**.

Inverse video. Also known as **reverse video**, this refers to **characters** which a computer can produce in negative. For example, light-coloured characters set on dark panels on a light-coloured screen, as on the screen above.

Wrap. This is the process by which the computer automatically starts a new line if a line of text is too long to fit onto one line of the screen.

Foreground and background. Sometimes known as **ink** and **paper**, these are, respectively, the colour that text is printed in, and the colour of the screen.

These are **inverse video characters**.

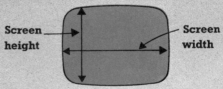

Screen displaying information from a computer.

Screen format. This is the number of **characters** which fit on a screen. It varies

Screen height

Screen width

from computer to computer. The **screen width** is the number of characters across a screen, and the **screen height** is the number down.

Types of screen

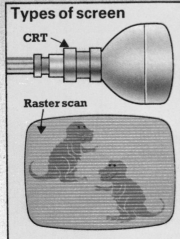

CRT

Raster scan

Cathode ray tube or **CRT.** This is the device inside a television which produces the beam of electrons that makes the picture on the screen.

Raster scan. This is the way that the beam of electrons produced by a CRT makes a screen picture. It scans back and forth across the screen from the top left-hand corner to the bottom right, far too fast to see, and constantly redraws the picture.

PAL. This is the standard for producing TV pictures in most of Western Europe. It stands for Phase Alternating Line and it defines how many lines per screen make up the **raster scan**, and how fast it scans.

NTSC. This is the TV picture standard in the USA, defining how many lines are scanned per screen, and how fast. NTSC stands for National Television Standard Committee.

Character matrix. Each **character** is displayed on the screen by lighting up dots in the shape of the character within a grid of dots, usually 8 by 8 or 7 by 8. This grid is called the **character matrix**.

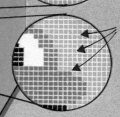

Character matrix

Pixels. These are the dots which the computer can light up to form pictures on the screen. Pixel is short for picture element.

Display modes

The term **mode** refers to a certain state of operation of a computer in which it can understand different commands. Most computers have several different **display modes**, enabling them to produce different kinds of display. In a **text mode** you can print general text on the screen – lines of data and programs, etc.

Some computers have a number of text modes in which they can print different numbers of **characters** across or down a screen, for example.

Teletext mode. In this mode, a computer can produce all the necessary **graphics** and **characters** to display computerized information sent with TV signals. *

Screen resolution. This refers to the number of **pixels** the computer can light up on the screen. It is also called **screen density**.

▲ **High resolution.** In high resolution, a computer can light up a large number of small pixels and make very detailed pictures.

For more about **pixels** and screen **graphics**, see pages 28 and 29.

▲ **Low resolution.** In low resolution, the pictures a computer can make are not very detailed because the pixels are quite large and there are fewer of them than in high resolution.

LCD

LCD. This stands for liquid crystal display – a way of producing a screen picture using a chemical which turns black when an electric current passes through it. Some small computers have **LCD screens**.

Monochrome. This is a one-colour or black-and-white screen. The single colour is usually green or amber.

RGB monitor. This is a special kind of colour **monitor**. Its display is made by three separate signals – one for each of the colours red, green and blue (RGB), which are the colours used to make a screen picture. This makes a clearer and sharper picture than the one combined signal used by a normal colour TV.

Luminosity. This is the brightness of a screen. Some screens have an **anti-glare** surface, making them easier to look at for long periods of time.

Teletext/viewdata compatible. This type of screen has the right **screen format** to be able to display **teletext** or **viewdata**.

9

*For more about **teletext** and **viewdata** see pages 26-27.

Memory and backing store

The **memory** is an area inside the computer where information and instructions are stored. It is sometimes known as **on-board memory**. The **backing store** consists of programs and data recorded on **cassettes** or **disks** (see pages 22-23), which can be copied back into the memory when needed. The computer's memory is divided into two areas – **RAM** and **ROM**.

RAM. This stands for **random access memory**. It is where the computer stores any information you give it. It is called random access memory because the computer can pick out, or **access**, any piece of data from any point.

Most RAM is **volatile**, which means that anything inside it is lost when the computer is switched off. This is why it is also called **temporary memory**. It can be either **static** or **dynamic**. Static RAM only receives an electrical pulse each time its contents need to be changed. Dynamic RAM needs to be continually refreshed with electrical pulses in order to retain its information.

ROM. This stands for **read only memory.** It is the area of the memory where the computer's own operating instructions are stored. This part of the memory cannot be used for storing any new information. ROM is **non-volatile**, which means that what it contains stays inside the computer whether it is switched on or off. It is often called **permanent memory.**

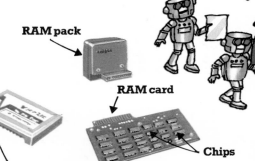

RAM pack

RAM card

Chips

RAM cartridge

For more memory words, see pages 18-19.

Memory expansion

To expand a computer's memory is to increase the size of its RAM so that you can use longer programs and store more information. You can expand the memory by plugging a **RAM pack** or **cartridge** into the **expansion port** on the computer, or by fitting a **RAM card** (a small **printed circuit board**) into a slot on the main circuit board inside the computer. Extra RAM is sometimes called **add-on RAM**.

Memory size

All information is sent to the memory as a code of electrical signals. There are two types of signal – pulse and no pulse. These are called **bits**, and all information received by the computer will end up in this form. Each letter, number or symbol is represented by a group of eight bits called a **byte**. The size of the memory is measured in **kilobytes** – one kilobyte is 1024 bytes, and is written as **1K** or **1Kbyte**. This is enough space for about 200 words. A **megabyte**, or **Mbyte**, is a million bytes.

Backing store

Any programs or data in the computer's RAM are lost when the computer is switched off. If you want to keep a copy, you must record the program or data on a **cassette** or **floppy disk**. You can also buy programs ready recorded. Any information stored externally like this is called **backing store**.

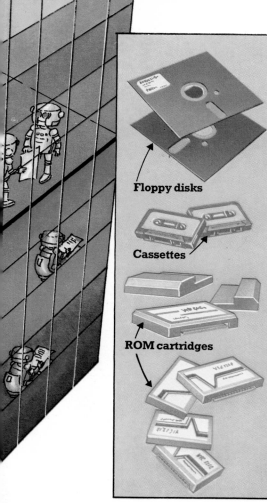

Floppy disks

Cassettes

ROM cartridges

Save. This is to record a program or data onto a cassette or disk.

Load. This is to transfer a program or data recorded on a cassette or disk back into the computer's memory.

Access time. This is the time the computer takes to find, or **access**, programs or data from a cassette or disk.

ROM cartridges. These contain permanent copies of programs. They slot into the back or side of the keyboard, and might contain games programs, for example, or instructions telling the computer how to make **graphics** or sounds.

Stringy floppy. This is a cartridge containing a continuous loop of magnetic tape on which you can record programs or data. It works almost as fast as a **floppy disk** (see page 22), but needs a special device to operate it.

Cassettes

Most **cassettes** used for storing programs and data are ordinary audio cassettes – the same kind as you use for recording music. You can also buy **data cassettes**, which are specially designed for recording computer signals.

A cassette contains a length of magnetic tape on which the computer signals are recorded as areas of varying magnetism. If you listen to a cassette on which a program is recorded, you can hear the signals as a series of high-pitched bleeps.

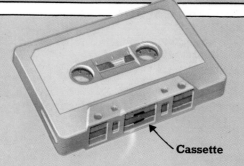

Cassette

Tape counter. This is a device built into most cassette recorders. It runs through the numbers from 0 to 9999 as a tape plays, and by setting it to 0 at the beginning of a tape, you can keep a note of where each program begins.

Leader. This is the clear or coloured plastic tape at the beginning of a cassette tape on which nothing can be recorded.

Header. This comes before a program or a block of data when you load it from a cassette. It gives the computer information about what it has loaded, such as the length of a block of data.

11

Inside the keyboard

A computer is a complex system of electrical **circuits.** Circuits are pathways along which an electric current can flow, and in a computer they carry the signals which represent data. Each set of circuits is known as an **integrated circuit, IC** or **chip**. The name chip comes from the tiny sliver of **silicon** out of which the circuits are made. The chips in a computer are fitted onto a **printed circuit board** or **PCB.** The picture on the right shows the printed circuit board of a microcomputer.

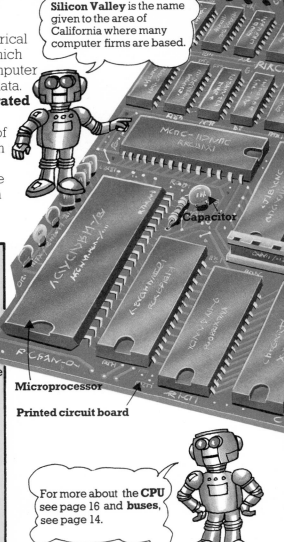

Silicon Valley is the name given to the area of California where many computer firms are based.

Capacitor

Microprocessor

Printed circuit board

Different kinds of chip

Microprocessor . This is the most important chip inside a microcomputer. Also sometimes known as the **MPU,** or microprocessor unit, it contains circuits which carry out the functions of the **central processing unit,** or **CPU.** This is the part that does all the work of the computer – carrying out instructions and controlling the flow of information.

Memory chips. These are the chips in which programs and data are stored. There are different chips for different kinds of memory (see below).

ROM chips. These are **read only memory** chips. They contain permanent copies of programs such as those which tell the computer how to carry out all the tasks it must be able to do.

RAM chips. These are **random access memory** chips and they are used to hold the programs and data which you put into the computer.

Input/output chips. These are also known as **I/O chips.** They control the flow of information between the computer and other equipment, such as a screen, a keyboard or a printer. I/O chips are used in **interfaces** (see page 15).

Dedicated chip. This is a chip which performs one task only, such as a memory chip.

For more about the **CPU** see page 16 and **buses,** see page 14.

Boards and buses

Printed circuit board or **PCB.** This is a board with thin metal tracks laid out on its surface, along which electric current can flow.

Edge connector. This is a place on the main printed circuit board where the tracks are brought right to the edge, so that such things as extra memory or program cartridges can be attached.

Bus. This is a set of tracks on a printed circuit board for carrying the computer signals between chips. There are several different buses for carrying different signals (see page 14).

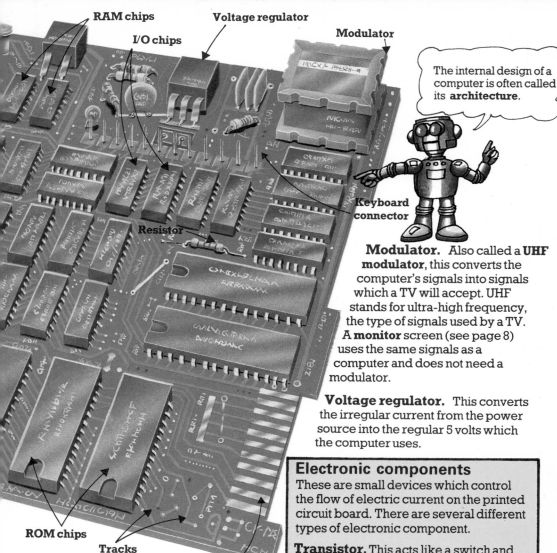

RAM chips

I/O chips

Voltage regulator

Modulator

The internal design of a computer is often called its **architecture**.

Resistor

Keyboard connector

ROM chips

Tracks

Edge connector

Modulator. Also called a **UHF modulator**, this converts the computer's signals into signals which a TV will accept. UHF stands for ultra-high frequency, the type of signals used by a TV. A **monitor** screen (see page 8) uses the same signals as a computer and does not need a modulator.

Voltage regulator. This converts the irregular current from the power source into the regular 5 volts which the computer uses.

Bus system. This refers to the lay-out of the tracks on a printed circuit board and the signals they carry. The **S100** is a well-known standard bus system.

Motherboard. This is a printed circuit board into which other boards, known as **daughterboards**, can be slotted and which can be attached to the side or back of a computer. The name is also sometimes given to the main circuit board inside a computer.

Card. This is a small printed circuit board, such as a daughterboard, which slots into the main circuit board. A card may carry extra memory chips, for example, or **interface** chips.

Electronic components

These are small devices which control the flow of electric current on the printed circuit board. There are several different types of electronic component.

Transistor. This acts like a switch and can stop the electric current or let it through. Transistors control the flow of pulse or no-pulse signals which the computer works with.

Diode. A diode allows electrical signals to pass through it in one direction only.

LED. This stands for light emitting diode. It is a diode made of special material which glows when an electric current passes through it. LEDs are often used as power on/off indicators.

Resistor. This controls the strength of the electric current.

Capacitor. This can store a small charge of current and is used to control and smooth the flow of electricity inside a computer.

13

Bits and bytes

Inside a computer, each piece of information takes the form of a number in **binary code**. This is a number system which uses only two digits, 1 and 0, to represent any number (see page 42).

The individual digits are called **bits**, short for binary digits, and they are represented by an electrical pulse for a 1 and no pulse for a 0. All the computer's work is done using streams of these pulses and no-pulses.

The pieces of data are represented by groups of eight bits called **bytes**. These are also called **words**. An **eight-bit computer** is one which works with **eight-bit words**, whereas a **16-bit computer** can carry out operations using **16-bit words**.

ASCII* codes. These are the standard code numbers for the letters, numbers and symbols that a computer uses. Each letter, number or symbol is represented by a byte of eight bits, although in fact only seven of these are the ASCII code. The leftmost bit is called the **parity bit**, and is used by the computer to check that the bits do not get changed accidentally when they are travelling from one part of the computer to another. If there is an odd number of 1s in the seven bits, the parity bit is set to 1, thus making the total number of 1s even. This is called **even parity**. You can also have **odd parity** where the bit is set to make the total number of 1s odd. The byte is checked at the receiving end against the parity bit.

Buses

The eight bits which make up each byte travel side by side, or **in parallel**, along eight tracks on the **printed circuit board** or inside the **chips**. Each of these groups of tracks is called a **bus**. There are different buses for different purposes.

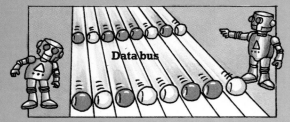

Data bus. This carries data, a byte at a time, between the **CPU** and the memory or a piece of external equipment, such as a printer.

Control bus. This carries signals from the **CPU** to control the various operations taking place. For instance, a signal is sent telling the memory whether a piece of data is to be stored there or taken out.

Address bus. These are the tracks used to carry **addresses** – the numbers which identify each place in the computer's memory. In an **eight-bit computer** (see above), the address bus has 16 parallel tracks, carrying 16 bits side by side in two bytes.

*For more about **ASCII**, see page 7.

Interfaces

An **interface** is a special piece of circuitry which handles the signals travelling between the computer and another piece of equipment, such as a cassette recorder or a printer. The interface converts the computer signals into signals suitable for the other piece of equipment and vice-versa. Interfaces for the most common equipment, such as a TV set or cassette recorder, are normally already built into a computer.

An interface also controls the speed at which data travels between the computer and external equipment. This is measured in **bits per second** (**bps**), and is called the **baud rate**. A **kilobaud** is a thousand bits per second.

If data is sent in a **synchronous** way, then the time intervals between the signals are regular. In **asynchronous** transmission, they are irregular, and special bits known as **start bits** and **stop bits** are also sent to indicate when one byte finishes and the next begins.

Types of interface

There are two main types of interface – **parallel** and **serial**. Inside the computer all the signals travel side by side, or in parallel, and a **parallel interface** is used to connect the computer to a piece of equipment which also works in parallel. A **serial interface** converts the computer's parallel signals into ones which travel one behind the other, or in serial, and vice-versa. They are used to connect the computer to pieces of equipment which work in serial. There are several standard interfaces (see below), which use internationally accepted voltage levels and wire arrangements inside the interfaces.

To computer

Serial signals

SERIAL INTERFACE

To computer

Parallel signals

PARALLEL INTERFACE

Standard interfaces

RS 232.* This is the most common type of serial interface. It is also known as **V24**.

RS423. This is a serial interface, a newer version of the **RS232**.

Centronics. This is a common parallel interface, used mainly to connect **printers**.

IEEE-488. This is a standard parallel interface. It is normally pronounced "I-triple E, 4 double 8".**

Handshaking. This term is used to describe the exchange of messages between a computer and external equipment, indicating that they are ready to send or receive data.

Upgrade. To upgrade a computer is to increase its capabilities. This can be done by adding extra **memory chips**, for example, or new **interfaces** in order to connect the computer to a wider range of equipment. Most computers are made in two versions: a basic version and an expanded one which has more memory and interfaces, etc. You can usually upgrade the basic version to the level of the expanded version.

15

*RS stands for Recommended Standard.

****IEEE** stands for the Institute of Electronic and Electrical Engineers.

Inside the CPU

The **CPU**, or **central processing unit**, is contained in a single **chip** called the **microprocessor** (see opposite). It is the part of the computer which performs all the operations needed to carry out a particular task. It is made up of three main parts – a set of **registers**, the **arithmetic and logic unit**, or **ALU**, and a **control unit**.

Registers

The registers are special storage spaces where data is held while the CPU is working on it. Most of the registers can hold one or two **bytes** and are used as "half-way houses" when data is being transferred between the CPU and the memory, but some, such as those below, also have special uses.

Accumulator. This register is used by the **ALU** for storing numbers being used in calculations.

Program counter. This holds the **address** in the memory where the next instruction to be carried out is stored.

Flag register. This is also called the **condition code register** or the **status register**. Each **bit** in this register is known as a **flag bit** and is used to record whether a particular condition has occurred. For example, one of the bits is called the **carry flag**. This is **set**, i.e. made equal to 1, if the result of the last calculation is too big to fit in a single **byte**.

Index register. The contents of this register are used when working out the **address** of the next piece of data to be used (see **indexed addressing**, page 39).

Stack pointer. This contains the **address** of the next free space in a **stack**, a special area of the memory.

Housekeeping. This refers to the tasks that the CPU carries out which are not directly related to solving a program problem. These include such things as dealing with the **input** and **output** of data.

Driver. This is a program which enables the CPU to control a piece of external equipment, e.g. search through a cassette or use a printer.

The ALU

The **ALU**, or **arithmetic and logic unit**, is the section of the CPU which does all the arithmetic. It can also make comparisons and choices.

Within the ALU, there are special electronic circuits called **gates**, or **logic gates**. These are made up of **transistors**, which can stop or send on the electric pulses that the computer works with. There are several different types of gate, and when they are put together in certain sequences they are able to carry out **binary** arithmetic (see page 42). The three main types are the **AND gate**, the **OR gate** and the **NOT gate**.

AND gate. This produces an electrical pulse (a "1") if it receives a pulse along each of its two input lines.

OR gate. This produces a pulse if it receives one along either, or both, of its input lines.

NOT gate. This only produces a pulse if its single incoming line carries no pulse.

Control unit

The control unit is the part of the CPU that controls and co-ordinates all the operations which are needed to complete one task, such as fetching data from the memory and sending it to the **ALU** to be worked on. It sends out **control signals** to set all these operations in motion and it co-ordinates them using a series of pulses generated by a **quartz crystal clock**. A computer's speed is measured by the number of these pulses its clock produces per second. One **megahertz** (MHz) is one million pulses per second.

Interrupt handler. Every so often (many times a second), the **control unit** sends a signal, called an **interrupt**, which makes the CPU stop what it is doing. The interrupt handler, one of the **operating system** programs, then gets the CPU to carry out its **interrupt routine**, which involves such things as scanning the keyboard to see if any keys have been pressed.

The operating system

All the instructions which tell the CPU how to carry out its various tasks are contained in special programs known as the **operating system, O/S** or **monitor**. They are stored in the permanent memory (**ROM**). Each make of computer has its own operating system which determines what it can do. Some makes of operating system, though, such as **CP/M** (Control Program/ Microprocessor) can be used in a number of different makes of computer, enabling them to run the same programs.

Bootstrap loader. If a computer's main **operating system** is not already in **ROM**, it must first be loaded before the computer can carry out even the most basic of tasks. This is done by a short program already in ROM called a bootstrap loader.

Types of microprocessor

There are a limited number of different types of microprocessor (see page 12), and between them they are used in virtually all the most common microcomputers. The type of microprocessor a computer has determines the set of machine code instructions (the **instruction set** – see page 38) that the CPU understands and the speed at which it operates. The improved versions of the microprocessors operate faster and understand more instructions.

6502 and 6510. These are made by **Mostek**, and are some of the most widely used microprocessors. The 6502 is used in the PET, the VIC 20 and the BBC, for example, and the 6510, an improved version of the 6502, is used in the Commodore 64.

Z80 and Z80A. These are made by **Zilog**. The Z80A is an improved version of the Z80, used, for example, in the Sinclair/Timex computers.

6800 and 6809. These are made by **Motorola**. The 6809 is an improved version of the 6800, and is used in the Dragon and the Tandy/Radio Shack Colour Computer.

More memory words

All the computer's memory – the **ROM** (read only memory) and the **RAM** (random access memory)* – is made up of lots of "boxes" called **memory locations**. Each location can hold one **byte**, that is, a group of eight electrical signals representing one piece of information.

Memory address. Each memory location has a number, called its **address**, so that the computer can find information again when it is needed. Each address is a **16-bit binary number**. This allows a microcomputer to have up to 65,536 (64**K**) different locations, numbered from 0 to 65,535 – the highest decimal number that can be represented by 16 binary digits.

Page. This is a term used to refer to a group of consecutive memory locations. The size of a page varies on different computers. On most microcomputers, it is 256 locations, on other computers it can be 512 or 1024 (one **kilobyte**).

The memory map

Different areas of the memory are used for different purposes and a diagram showing the areas and their addresses is called a **memory map**. A memory map of some kind is normally included in a computer's manual. Some of the different areas are shown on the right and listed below.

User RAM. This is the area of **RAM** in which your programs and data are stored. You cannot use all of RAM because the computer takes over some of it for its own use when you switch it on.

Screen memory. This is a group of consecutive memory locations, also called the **graphics page** or **display file**, which are used to store information to be displayed on the screen. Each memory location represents one position on the screen and the display is known as a **memory-mapped display**. You can change what is displayed by changing the contents of the individual locations.

Display attributes file. These memory locations hold extra information, called **display attributes**, about the **graphics** or **characters** displayed on the screen, e.g. their colour or whether they are in **inverse video**.

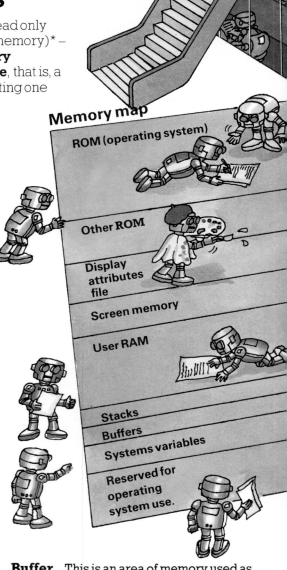

Memory map

ROM (operating system)

Other ROM

Display attributes file

Screen memory

User RAM

Stacks

Buffers

Systems variables

Reserved for operating system use.

Buffer. This is an area of memory used as a "half-way house" to hold information travelling either between different parts of the computer, or between the computer and a piece of external equipment. Some examples of buffers are a keyboard buffer and a cassette buffer.

Reserved for operating system use. This is used by the computer's own operating programs (the **operating system** – see page 17) for storing the information it needs to do its work. In some computers, the **buffers, stacks** and **systems variables** are all included in this area of the memory map.

18

*For more about **ROM** and **RAM**, see page 10.

Any area of memory where the **CPU** temporarily stores data is called **scratch pad memory**.

FFFF

E000

C000

BC00

HIMEM   B400

These are memory addresses in **hex**. For more about hex, see page 42.

1000

C00

800

200

0000

PEEK and POKE

If you want to deal directly with particular **memory locations**, you can use the **BASIC** commands **PEEK** and **POKE**, together with the **address** in memory that you want to deal with.

PEEK. This tells the computer to "peek into", or read the contents of, a memory location. You can PEEK any location in the memory.

POKE. This tells the computer to store a piece of information in a memory location. You can POKE any **RAM** location, but you may disrupt the working of the system if you POKE some parts of it, e.g. the **systems variables**. If you do, you can restore the computer to normal by switching it off and on again.

HIMEM. Also known as the top of memory, or **RAMTOP**, this is the highest **address** in **user RAM**, that is, the highest address at which your information can be stored.

Queue. This term is given to any area of memory used for storing data according to the **FIFO** principle – "first in, first out", just like any queue, in fact.

Systems variables. This area of the memory is used by the computer to hold constantly varying information, such as the position of the **cursor** on the screen and the **address** of the next free space in **user RAM**.

Stack. This is a section of memory used for storing data in a particular way. It works on the **LIFO** principle, or "last in, first out". The last piece of data stored will be the first to be retrieved.

There are several different stacks, used for different purposes, e.g. the **GOSUB stack**, which holds the program line numbers to be returned to after subroutines in a program, the **calculator stack**, which holds intermediate results during calculations, and the **machine stack** or **processor stack**, which the **CPU** uses for holding various information, such as the point in a program to return to after an **interrupt** (see page 17).

Other kinds of memory

Virtual memory. Some computers can store and retrieve information on **disks** as though the disks were part of the memory, that is, without needing commands from the user. This extra "pretend" memory is called virtual memory.

RAM disks. These are a fairly new development. They are not really disks at all, but sets of **RAM chips** which the computer treats like disks. It needs a command to fetch information from them, but the process is much faster than with a disk.

Bubble memory. These are special **chips** which store information as tiny "bubbles" of magnetism. They are also a new development. They can store much more data than a silicon chip and retain it when the power is switched off. Bubble memory is slower than ordinary memory, though.

19

Peripherals

A **peripheral** is any piece of equipment which you can connect to a computer. It is also known as an **add-on device**. Two of the most common peripherals are a **cassette recorder** and a **disk drive**, both of which are used for storing data and programs.

In order to connect a peripheral to a computer you need an **interface**. This is a special piece of circuitry that converts and controls the signals between the computer and the peripheral so that they can understand each other.[*]

An **input/output device**, or **I/O device**, is any peripheral which is used to feed, or **input**, data into a computer, or which uses data it receives from the computer (**output**) to perform some task. Below are some of the most common.

Digital tracer ▼ This is also known as a **digitizer**. It is a special hinged arm which you can use to trace over drawings and graphs and which sends the information to the computer for drawing out on the screen.

Light pen ▶ This is a pen-like instrument which you connect to a computer and use to draw directly on the screen or to choose an option by pointing at it on the screen.

Light pen

Graphics tablet ▼ This is also known as a **digitizing pad, digitizer** or **bit pad.** You draw on the tablet and it sends signals to the computer to display your drawing on the screen.

Mouse

Digital tracer

Mouse ▲ This is a small device with wheels which is used to input data by tracing over graphs, etc., or to indicate in which direction a computer should move a pointer on the screen.

Analogue (analog) to digital converter. The data sent by some peripherals to a computer takes the form of varying levels of electrical voltage. An **analogue to digital converter**, or **A/D converter**, translates these voltage levels into the pulse or no-pulse signals, known as **digital signals**, which the computer uses. A similar piece of equipment, called a **digital to analogue (D/A) converter**, does the opposite job.

Modem. This stands for modulator/demodulator. It is a device which allows you to send and receive computer signals along the telephone lines. It does this by converting the computer signals into phone signals, or vice-versa. A modem may be built into a special telephone or it may take the form of an **acoustic coupler** (see right).

Graphics tablet

Acoustic coupler ▼ This is a portable **modem**, often just known as a modem, which can be connected to a computer and used with any telephone. You place the telephone handset into the coupler and it converts the signals travelling to or from the computer.

Telephone handset

Acoustic coupler

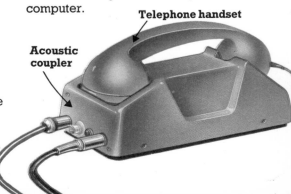

*For more about **interfaces**, see page 15.

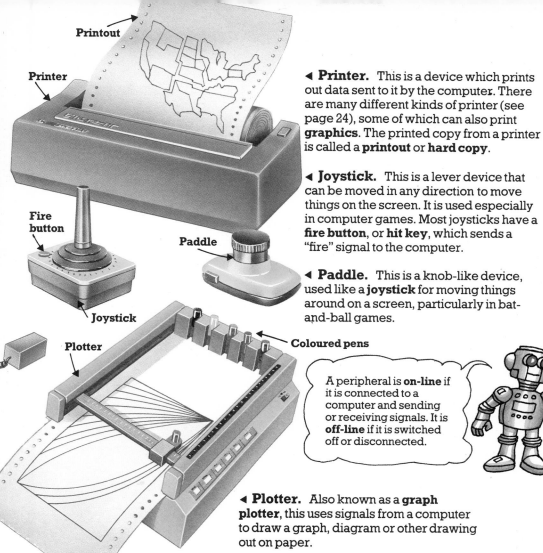

Printout

Printer

Fire button

Paddle

Joystick

Plotter

Coloured pens

◄ **Printer.** This is a device which prints out data sent to it by the computer. There are many different kinds of printer (see page 24), some of which can also print **graphics**. The printed copy from a printer is called a **printout** or **hard copy**.

◄ **Joystick.** This is a lever device that can be moved in any direction to move things on the screen. It is used especially in computer games. Most joysticks have a **fire button**, or **hit key**, which sends a "fire" signal to the computer.

◄ **Paddle.** This is a knob-like device, used like a **joystick** for moving things around on a screen, particularly in bat-and-ball games.

A peripheral is **on-line** if it is connected to a computer and sending or receiving signals. It is **off-line** if it is switched off or disconnected.

◄ **Plotter.** Also known as a **graph plotter**, this uses signals from a computer to draw a graph, diagram or other drawing out on paper.

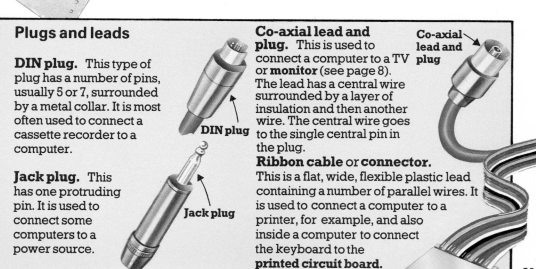

Plugs and leads

DIN plug. This type of plug has a number of pins, usually 5 or 7, surrounded by a metal collar. It is most often used to connect a cassette recorder to a computer.

Jack plug. This has one protruding pin. It is used to connect some computers to a power source.

Co-axial lead and plug. This is used to connect a computer to a TV or **monitor** (see page 8). The lead has a central wire surrounded by a layer of insulation and then another wire. The central wire goes to the single central pin in the plug.

Ribbon cable or **connector.** This is a flat, wide, flexible plastic lead containing a number of parallel wires. It is used to connect a computer to a printer, for example, and also inside a computer to connect the keyboard to the **printed circuit board**.

DIN plug

Jack plug

Co-axial lead and plug

Disks and disk drives

Floppy disks, also called **flexible disks** or **diskettes**, are thin plastic disks on which computer programs and data can be stored. The programs and data are recorded onto a disk, or read off it, in a **disk drive**.

Disk controller. This tells the computer how to work the disk drive. It can be either a small **printed circuit board** or extra **chips**.

Disk interface. This controls the signals travelling between the computer and the disk drive.*

Disk operating system. Often shortened to **DOS** (pronounced "doss"), this is a group of programs which tell the computer how to read and store information on a disk. Some computers have a disk operating system already in **ROM**, others have a short program which knows just enough to load the main DOS from a disk. This is called **booting DOS**.

Ribbon connector

Some computers have these built in, but you usually have to add them.

Disk slides in here

Disk controller

Types of disk

Floppy disks can be either **single-sided** (**SS**), which means you can record onto one side only, or **double-sided** (**DS**). Data is recorded onto disks as patterns of magnetic dots and **disk density** refers to the amount of data which can be recorded on a disk. **Double-density** (**DD**) disks can store twice as much data as **single-density** (**SD**) disks.

Minifloppies. These are 5¼ inches in diameter and can hold at least 100 **kilobytes**, depending on the **density** (see above) of the disk. Most microcomputers use minifloppy disks, which are usually just referred to as floppy disks.

Microfloppies. These are between 3″ and 4″ in diameter and different makes hold different amounts of data.

Standard floppies. These are 8″ in diameter and are used mainly on large computers.

Hard disks. These are made of hard non-flexible material. A typical 5¼″ hard disk can store at least 5 **megabytes**. They are used mainly on large computers.

Floppy disk

Head access window

Disk is kept permanently inside protective envelope.

Tracks are rings round the disk.

Tracks

Disk

Sector

Formatting a disk

Before you use a disk it must be **formatted** or **initialized**, that is, divided up into **tracks** and **sectors**. This is done by one of the programs in the disk operating system. A minifloppy is usually divided into 40 tracks, or 80 if it is **double-tracked**, and 10 or 16 sectors. **Hard sectored** disks already have their sectors marked, **soft sectored** ones are divided into sectors and tracks by the program. The computer keeps a record of the tracks and sectors and uses it to find the different blocks of data or programs stored on the disk.

Sectors are slices made by lines from the centre to the outside edge of the disk.

*For more about **interfaces**, see page 15.

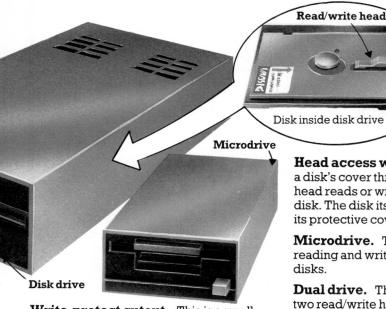

Read/write head. This passes over the surface of the spinning disk and either reads or writes information on it.

Read/write head

Disk inside disk drive

Microdrive

Disk drive

Head access window. This is the hole in a disk's cover through which the read/write head reads or writes information on the disk. The disk itself is never removed from its protective cover.

Microdrive. This is a small disk drive for reading and writing from microfloppy disks.

Dual drive. This is a disk drive which has two read/write heads and can hold two disks.

Drive spec. Most microcomputers can operate more than one disk drive, and the drive spec, or drive specification, is the instruction you give the computer telling it which one to use.

Write-protect cutout. This is a small notch on the disk's cover which shows you can record onto the disk. If it is covered with a tab of tape, or not there at all, then you cannot record on the disk. This is to stop you recording over data by accident.

Write-protect cutout

Files
A **file** is a package of programs or data stored under one name on a disk or a cassette.

Data file. This is a file containing data rather than programs. If the data is text, e.g. words and sentences, it is a **text file.**

Random access file. Also called a **direct access file**, this is a file which is arranged so that the computer can find, or **access**, any piece of data straight away wherever it is in the file. This contrasts with **sequential**, or **serial, access files**, which the computer has to search through from the beginning.

Records and fields. Files can be divided into records and fields to make the data easier to find and change. For example, a file holding details about different makes of computer would be split into a record for each make of computer. These records would be subdivided into fields, each holding one piece of information about a particular make, such as its memory size.

Disk directory or **catalog.** This is the computer's own record of where each file or program is stored on the disk. The directory usually takes up a few tracks at the beginning of a disk.

Back-up disk. A disk with copies of data already recorded on another disk is known as a back-up disk. It is kept as a safety measure in case the original disk is accidentally erased.

Protected file. This is also known as a **locked file**. A computer will only load the data it holds if you give the right password. This is to make sure that only people with the right to see the data can obtain access to it.

File handling. This refers to the manipulation of files by a computer and includes such things as sorting through and deleting data.

Disk filing system. Often known as a **DFS**, this is simply a collection of files held on one or more disks – a computerized version of a filing cabinet.

Printers

A **printer** is a piece of equipment which can print out paper copies of programs and data from the computer's memory. There are many different kinds of printer which use different methods to print the data out on the paper. Most inexpensive printers are **serial printers**, or **character printers**, which means they print one **character** at a time. A **line printer** also prints each character in turn, but so fast that it is regarded as printing one line at once.

Bit image printing

Sprocket holes

Printout

Sprockets

Platen

Printer

Print head

Types of printer

Impact printer. This is any printer which prints the **characters** by hitting an ink-coated ribbon against the paper, like an ordinary typewriter. Some examples of impact printers, each of which uses a different **print head**, are a **dot matrix printer**, a **daisywheel printer** and a **thimble printer**.

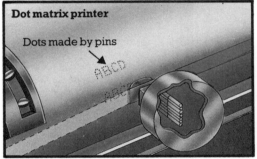

Dot matrix printer

Dots made by pins

Dot matrix printer ▲ The print head is a set of fine pins and it prints a character by hitting the ribbon with the group of pins which make up the shape of that character.

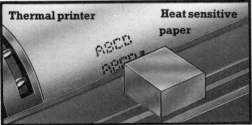

Thermal printer

Heat sensitive paper

Thermal printer ▲ This uses special heat-sensitive paper and burns the shapes of the characters onto it.

Electrosensitive printer. This is also called a **spark printer**. It is like a thermal printer but the paper is aluminium-coated and sparks of electricity burn the characters onto it.

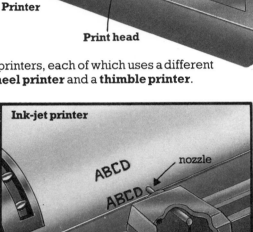

Ink-jet printer

nozzle

Ink-jet printer ▲ This prints the characters by directing very fine jets of electrically-charged ink at the paper.

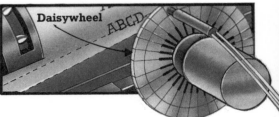

Daisywheel

Daisywheel printer ▲ This has a disk called the **daisywheel** or **printwheel** with characters round the edge. The disk is rotated until it is in the right position for a character to be hit against the ribbon.

Thimble printer. This is like a daisywheel printer, but the characters are around the edge of a thimble-shaped print head.

Printout. This is also known as **hard copy**. It is the **output** of a computer printed on paper. There are a number of different kinds of paper and some printers are able to use more than one kind (see next page).

Bit image mode. Some printers can print both text and **graphics**. When a printer is in bit image mode, it prints patterns of dots to make graphics.

Platen. This is the roller or cylinder around which the paper is guided.

Carriage return. This is the process by which the **print head** is returned to the starting point for the next line.

Print head. This is the part of a printer which does the printing. It might be a **daisywheel**, for example, or a nozzle which fires jets of ink.

Sprockets. These are pins which fit into the **sprocket holes** in **fanfold paper** (see next page) and pull the paper through.

Bi-directional printing. With this kind of printing, the **print head** moves from side to side across the paper, printing the first line from left to right, the next from right to left, and so on. This saves greatly on printing time.

Logic-seeking. **Bi-directional printers** are logic-seeking, that is, they decide which is the fastest way to print the next line according to the length of the line they have just finished and that of the one to follow.

Printer buffer. This is a special part of the computer's or printer's memory which holds the data on its way to be printed. This is necessary because the computer sends data much faster than the printer can print it out.

cps. This stands for **characters per second**. It is a measurement of the speed of a printer. A typical dot matrix printer prints at a rate of about 80cps.

The characters

Typeface. This is the design of a printer's set of characters.

PRINT

PRINT

Double-width characters. Also called **expanded** or **enlarged characters**, these are twice the width of normal ones.

PRINT

Condensed characters. These are narrower than normal.

Subscript and **superscript.** These are small letters or numbers printed below (subscript) or above (superscript) the line.

$Y_2 = X_1 + X_3$

$5^2 + 3^3 = 52$

Proportional spacing. Some printers can vary the space taken up by each letter, so that an "i", for instance, is narrower than an "m". This is called proportional spacing. On other printers, all the letters are the same width.

PRINT

PRINT

True and **false descenders.** **Descenders** are the "tails" of letters like "p" and "g". Some printers have true descenders, which project below the line, but with others, the "tails" finish exactly on the line. These are false descenders.

Emphasized characters. These are printed darker than normal, so that they stand out.

graphics

graphics

Printer paper

Printer paper can come in one of two main ways – as individual sheets, known as **cut paper**, or as one long sheet, in which case it is called **continuous stationery**. There are two main types of continuous stationery: **fanfold paper** and **roll paper**.

Fanfold paper. Also called **concertina fold** and **accordion fold**, this type of paper is divided into pages by lines of perforations. The pages are folded first in one direction and then the other and piled in a block.

Roll paper. This comes as a roll which must be put on a special holder.

Feeding

The process of moving the paper up as lines are printed is known as **feeding**.

Friction feed. With this method, the paper is gripped between the **platen** and a set of smaller rollers.

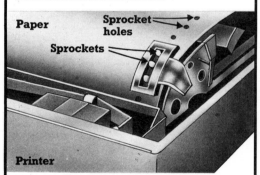

Paper

Sprocket holes

Sprockets

Printer

Pin feed. This is also known as **tractor feed** or **sprocket feed**. Each end of the **platen** has a ring of pins, called **sprockets**, sticking up round the edge. These pins pass through **sprocket holes** down the side of the paper and pull it through the printer.

Line feed. This rolls the paper up one line at the end of each line of printing.

Form feed. This is the process by which **continuous stationery** is rolled up to the start of a new page.

Reverse feed. Some printers can move the paper down as well as up. This is called reverse feed. It is particularly useful for printing **graphics**.

Databases

A **database*** or **databank** is a large store of information held in a central computer. The information can be made available either to a select number of people or to the public in general. The databases with only limited access hold such information as vehicle licence numbers, criminal records and secret government files. Those which are available for anyone to use contain all kinds of information – from sports results, cookery hints and weather reports to financial news and economic forecasts.

Using a database

There are several different ways of receiving information from a database. A computer can be connected to the database computer by cables, or the information can be sent as TV signals or via the telephone lines. If it is sent as TV signals, it is known as **teletext** and if it travels along the phone lines it is called **viewdata**. Together these are known as **videotex**.

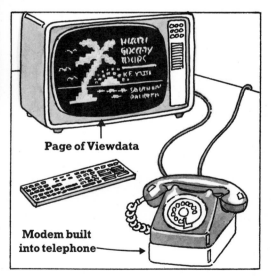

Page of Viewdata

Modem built into telephone

Viewdata. This is information sent as signals over a telephone line and displayed as text on a TV screen. To receive viewdata you need a device called a **modem** (see page 20) to decode the signals. Depending on the system, this could be built into the TV or the telephone, or it could be connected or built into a computer.

*See also page 37.

Telecomputing. This refers to the sending and receiving of information between computers over long distances, via the telephone lines or TV signals. Computer programs sent in this way are known as **telesoftware** and to load them into a computer is called **downloading**.

This is an example of the kind of information sent by **teletext** or **viewdata**.

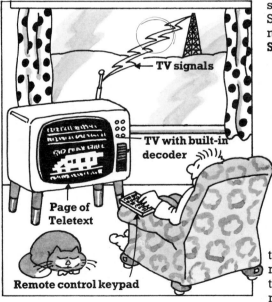

Page of Teletext

TV signals

TV with built-in decoder

Remote control keypad

Teletext. This is information sent alongside normal TV programme signals from a central database to a TV set. No computer is needed, but the TV set must have a built-in decoder to convert the signals it receives into screens full of text, known as **pages**. Each page has its own number, and you select the page you want by typing its number on a remote control keypad.

Networks

A **network** is a group of computers which are linked together by special cables or via the telephone lines, so that they can pass information to each other or share equipment.

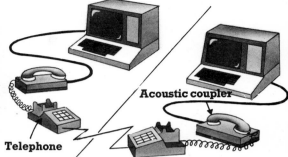

Acoustic coupler

Telephone

A **home computer network** is one in which home users can communicate with each other by sending messages and programs via the phone lines. Some groups may buy space on a central viewdata-type system, so that they can use its facilities as well. Some examples of home computer networks are **Micronet** in the UK and **The Source** and **CompuServe** in the USA.

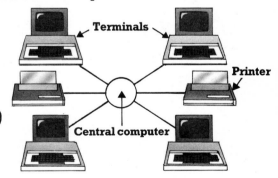

Terminals

Printer

Central computer

Businesses often set up networks in order to communicate with each other. A business network may link several computers together, or a central computer and a number of **terminals** and other pieces of equipment. A terminal may be just a keyboard and screen used to exchange information with the central computer, or it may be able to process its own data, in which case it is called an **intelligent terminal**. A network with one central computer and a number of terminals is known as a **multi-access system** because several people can use the computer at once. This is called **time-sharing.**

Graphics words

The term **graphics** is used to describe any pictures or diagrams drawn by a computer. The graphics can be displayed on a screen or printed out on a **printer** or **plotter**.

How computers make graphics

Graphics, like letters and numbers, are displayed on the screen by lighting up tiny dots called **pixels**. The quality of the pictures a computer can produce depends largely on how many of these pixels it can light up on the screen.

Pixels. This stands for picture elements.. These are the dots on the screen which light up to make pictures. Some computers can change the size of the dots, and make pictures with different degrees of detail, or **resolution** (see below).

High resolution graphics. A computer which can light up a large number of small pixels can produce very detailed pictures, known as high resolution graphics, or **hi-res graphics.** On a typical home computer, this is about 40,000 pixels, although computers with specialized high resolution graphics programs can light up many more.

Low resolution graphics. These are pictures made with a small number of quite large pixels, also called **low-res graphics.** The shapes in the pictures have jagged rather than smooth edges and are not very detailed.

Graphics mode. On some computers, you have to change to a graphics mode before you can program them to make pictures. Most computers have several different graphics modes, with different **resolutions**, for example, or a different number of colours.

Window. You can program some computers to produce an area called a window anywhere on the screen, in which you can display text on a graphics screen, or vice-versa.

Display attributes. The **attributes** of a graphics display are such things as the colour of its various parts, or whether they are in **inverse video** or flashing (**blinking**). This information is stored as **display attribute bytes** in the memory.*

Palette. This is the range of colours a computer can produce on the screen.

Graphics commands

These are the words which you use to tell a computer to draw pictures, such as DRAW and PLOT. The words vary on different computers.

Plot. This means to light up a **pixel**. To do this, you give the computer a graphics command and the **co-ordinates** of the pixel. These are two numbers which indicate its position on the screen. The **x co-ordinate** gives the number of pixels across the screen and the **y co-ordinate** is the number up, or on some computers, down the screen. **Absolute co-ordinates** are measured from the bottom left-hand, or top left-hand, corner of the screen. **Relative co-ordinates** are measured from the last point plotted on the screen.

DRAW 5,5

For more about **pixels** and **screen resolution**, see page 9.

Window

*For more about this, see **display attributes file**, page 18.

Different kinds of graphics

Graphics characters. These are small shapes which take up the same space as a normal character, i.e. a letter or number. Some computers have them on the keys and you can use them to make pictures or decorate programs. The group of graphics characters available on a particular computer is known as its **graphics set**. You may also be able to make up your own character-sized graphics – these are called **user-defined graphics characters**.

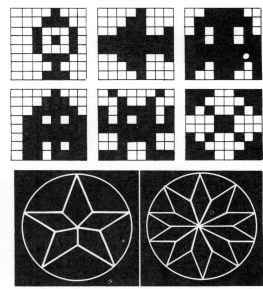

Line graphics. These are pictures which are produced by programming a computer to draw lines to certain points on the screen from other points. The computer automatically lights up all the dots along the line.

Turtle graphics. This is a method of producing pictures by moving an arrowhead round the screen. The arrowhead is called a **turtle** and you can instruct it to turn through angles and move certain distances or to certain points, either drawing or not drawing a line.

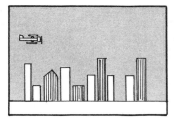
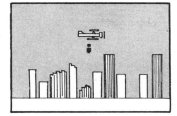
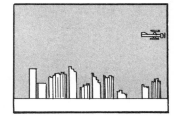

Animated graphics. These are pictures or shapes which move across the screen. The moving effect is created by plotting the shapes in one position and then deleting them and plotting them at the next position along or down the screen. Some specialized graphics programs can work out all the positions, or **frames**, between two points and display them automatically. This is called **inbetweening**.

Sprites. These are figures in a graphic display which can be programmed by name to appear at any point on the screen and to move around. They are often larger than **graphics characters** and can be made to move in front of, or behind, other sprites.

CAD. This stands for **Computer Aided Design**. CAD programs are available to help professional designers produce their designs. CAD is also being used more and more in industry as an aid to the design of various products.

3D graphics. This refers to screen pictures which give the illusion of being solid, or three-dimensional (3D). The simplest 3D picture is called a **wire-frame drawing**. All the lines which make up the picture are shown, even if they would be hidden if the object really were solid.

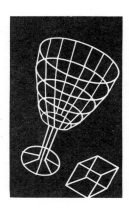

Computer languages

A **computer language**, also called **programming language**, is a set of words, numbers and symbols which you must use when you give a computer instructions. There are lots of different computer languages, many specially designed for carrying out specific tasks. Languages which use words similar to our own language are called **high-level languages. Low-level languages** are closer to the computer's own **binary code** (see page 14). There are two main types of low-level language, **machine code** and **assembly language**, although programming in either is usually known as **machine code programming.***

Interpreters and compilers

High-level languages have to be translated into the computer's own code by a special program which may be either an **interpreter** or a **compiler**. The difference between the two lies in the way they translate a program.

When you run a program, an **interpreter** takes one instruction at a time, translates it and then carries it out. A **compiler** translates all the instructions first, and then carries them out. Compiled programs run much faster than interpreted ones.

Most home computers have a **BASIC interpreter** built into their **ROM**. If you want to use any other language, you can usually load an interpreter or compiler for that language into your computer's memory.

Nearly all versions of **BASIC** use an **interpreter**, but you can get **BASIC compilers** for some micros.

INTERPRETER

Source code. This is the language a program is written in.

Object code. This is the code that a computer translates a program into.

High-level languages

BASIC. This stands for Beginner's All-purpose Symbolic Instruction Code. It is easily the most popular high-level language, although programs written in BASIC are not as concise and do not run as fast as those in some other languages. Different makes of computer use their own version of BASIC, with slightly different words and rules. These versions are called **dialects**. Some examples are **BBC BASIC, Microsoft BASIC** (or **M-BASIC**) and **Sinclair BASIC**.

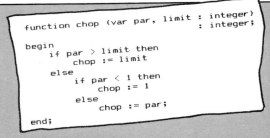

```
function chop (var par, limit : integer)
                               : integer;

begin
     if par > limit then
          chop := limit
     else
          if par < 1 then
               chop := 1
          else
               chop := par;

end;
```

```
10 REM - A BASIC PROGRAM
20 PRINT "WHO ARE YOU?";
30 INPUT N$
40 PRINT "HELLO, ";N$;
50 PRINT "NICE TO MEET YOU!"
```

A version of BASIC in which you cannot use all the possible instructions of the language is called **Tiny BASIC**, and one with more instructions, or a more versatile way of using them, is called **Extended BASIC.**

Pascal. This language is named after the 17th century French mathematician and scientist, Blaise Pascal, and first appeared in the 1960s. It can deal with a wide range of problems and its programs are **structured**, or set out logically in blocks. It is quite an involved language to learn.

PILOT. This is one of the languages developed for writing **CAI** (Computer Assisted Instruction) or **CAL** (Computer Assisted Learning) programs. These are programs used to teach various subjects.

30

*For more about **machine code programming**, see page 38.

Low-level languages

Each task a computer performs is made up of lots of small operations, each represented by one or more groups of eight signals called **bytes**. In a **high-level language**, one program instruction sets off a chain of operations for one task but in **low-level languages**, you have to give the computer an instruction for each of the operations. Low-level programs run at least ten times faster than high-level ones, though.

Machine code

The term machine code, or machine language, is sometimes used to mean the computer's own **binary code** (see page 14), into which all programs are finally converted. More generally, though, it refers to programs which are written in the **hex** equivalent of this binary code. **Hex**, short

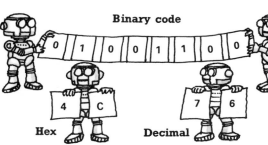

Binary code

| 0 | 1 | 0 | 0 | 1 | 1 | 0 | 0 |

Hex — 4 C

Decimal — 7 6

for **hexadecimal**, is a number system which uses 16 digits – the figures 0 to 9 and the letters A to F. It works like a decimal system, except that you count up to 15 before making a new column.

Assembly language

This is another way of writing a program in **low-level language**. The instructions you give the computer for each operation are written as **mnemonics**, which are English-like abbreviations, such as LD for load or JMP for jump.

JMP — Assembly language = 01001100 Computer code

JMP — Disassembler = 01001100 Computer code

Assembly language programs need a special program called an **assembler** to convert the language into the code used by the computer. This may be built into the computer, or you may have to load it separately. A **disassembler** converts the program in the computer's memory back into assembly language if you want to list it on the screen, for example.

```
: CUBE          ( OF TOP ITEM ON STACK)
  DUP           ( READY TO PRINT ARGUMENT)
  CR 3 .R       ( PRINT IT!)
  DUP DUP * *   ( CUBE IT)
  6 .R          ( AND PRINT THE RESULT)
;
```

FORTH. Designed for use on small computers, this language allows you to make up your own operations, programming words or structures. Its programs take up very little memory space.

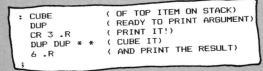

```
1-02-00-UPDATE-FILES SECTION.
1-02-00-ENTER
        READ VALID TRANSACTIONS
             AT END MOVE 1 TO EOT-FLAG.
        IF TRANSACTIONS-PROCESSED
             NEXT SENTENCE
        ELSE
             IF HEADER
                  NEXT SENTENCE
             ELSE
                  PERFORM 2-02-00-
                  TRANSACTIONS-PROCESS.
1-02-99-EXIT.
        EXIT.
```

COBOL. This stands for COmmon Business Oriented Language. It is a language used for processing business data – files, lists, etc.

```
C         REAL FUNCTION DOUBLE (NUMBER)
C
C         THIS FUNCTION DOUBLES ITS ARGUMENT

          REAL NUMBER
          DOUBLE = 2.0 * NUMBER
          RETURN
          END
```

FORTRAN. This stands for FORmula TRANslation. The language was invented in the 1950s and is the most commonly used of the languages developed for scientific and mathematical work. It is not as good as some languages at handling words. The most recent version is known as **FORTRAN 77.**

```
TO PINWHEEL
REPEAT 8 [RIGHT 45 BOX]
RIGHT 180
FORWARD 50
END
```

LOGO. This language was developed especially for teaching mathematical ideas to young children. It is the language used to give instructions to a small robot called a **turtle.**

31

Programming words

A computer **program** is a list of instructions written in a language that the computer understands and which tells it how to carry out a particular task. As well as instructions, you must also give the computer information to work on. This is called **data**.

The most common ways of giving a computer a program are by typing on the keyboard or loading it from a cassette or disk. The computer then stores the program in its memory until you tell it to **run** the program, that is, carry out the instructions.

Listing. This is a copy of all the lines of a program, either displayed on the screen or printed out on paper.

Instruction and **command.** In a program line such as GOTO 20, the keyword GOTO is a command, and the whole line is an instruction.

Multistatement line. This is a program line containing more than one **instruction.**

Keywords. These are the words in a **programming language** (see page 30), such as PRINT and INPUT in BASIC. Each word sets off a chain of operations inside the computer. Keywords are also called **reserved words.**

Direct instruction or **command.** This is an **instruction** or **command** which is not part of a program. It is carried out immediately.

> This is a program in BASIC.

Listing →

Line numbers

Multistatement line

Keywords

```
10 REM - A BASIC PROGRAM
20 INPUT N$
30 IF N$="FRED" THEN
   PRINT "HELLO":STOP
40 PRINT "GO AWAY"
50 GOTO 20
RUN
```

Direct command

Statement

Program planning

Flow chart. This is a diagram which is often used in the planning of a computer program. It shows the sequence of steps needed to solve a problem.

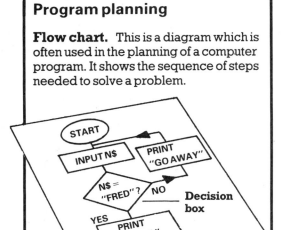

START → INPUT N$ → PRINT "GO AWAY"

N$ = "FRED"? NO — **Decision box**

YES → PRINT "HELLO" → STOP — **Instruction box**

Errors

An error in a program is called a **bug**. If an error is in the use of the programming language, then it is called a **syntax error**. This may be a spelling mistake, for example. When there is a bug in a program, the computer usually lets you know with an **error message** or a **report code**. An error message normally tells you what kind of bug it is, whereas a report code gives you a code which you look up in your manual.

Debugging. This means getting rid of a bug.

Crash. If a computer stops working suddenly and does not respond to anything you type on the keyboard, it is said to have crashed. A crash can be caused by a number of different things. Normally the only way to get the computer working again is to switch it off and start again, or press the **reset** button.

Glitch or **spike.** This is an electrical fault caused by uneven current. It may cause bugs in a program, or erase the program completely.

Variables

A variable is a label given to a piece of data in a computer program. For example, the statement LET C = 8 gives the variable C a value of 8. The value of the variable may change many times during a program.

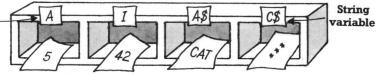

Numeric variable

String variable

Numeric variable. This is a variable whose values are always numbers. In BASIC, the variable is usually a letter such as A or I.

Integer variable. The changing values of an integer variable are always whole numbers, or **integers**. This type of variable is indicated by a % sign in BASIC.

Floating point variable. The values given to this type of variable are **floating point**, or **real numbers**, that is, ones with figures after the decimal point.

String variable. This is a variable which can be used for letters and symbols as well as numbers. It is indicated by a $ sign in BASIC , e.g. C$. This is called "C string" or "C dollar". A **null string** is one which contains nothing.

Array. An array is a group of related pieces of data stored together in the memory under one label. Each piece of data, known as an **element**, is referred to by this label and the number of its position in the array. This number is called its **subscript**. A **string array** is an array containing letters or symbols, and its label has a $ sign in BASIC.

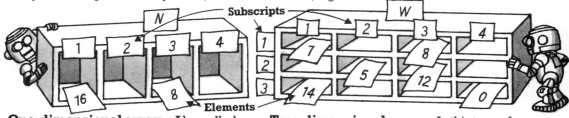

Subscripts

Elements

One-dimensional array. Also called a **vector**, this is an array where each piece of data has just one **subscript**. Four numbers stored in an array N, for example, would be called N(1), N(2), N(3) and N(4), and might be the ages of four people. Their names would be stored in a string array, e.g. M$.

Two-dimensional array. In this type of array, also called a **matrix**, the data is arranged in rows and columns and each piece has two **subscripts**: its row and column numbers. For example, W(2,3) is the third item in the second row of an array W.

Doing things with variables

Set. To set a variable is to give it a value. This is also called **assigning a value** to a variable, and a statement such as LET A = 40 is an **assignment statement**.

Clear. This means to make the value of a variable equal to 0.

Initialize. This is to give a variable a starting value, or **initial value**.

Dimension an array. This is to tell a computer the number and arrangement of items in an **array**. In BASIC, this is done using the command DIM and the array name and number of **elements**, e.g. DIM N(10).

Increment. This is to increase the value of a variable, usually by one, e.g. LET A = A + 1.

Decrement. This is to decrease a variable's value, usually by one, e.g. LET B = B − 1.

More programming words

A computer can carry out three main tasks: following an instruction, making a decision and repeating an operation. These tasks are the basis of all programs, and they are all used in the BASIC program on the right. These two pages explain some of the main structures used in BASIC programs.

Conditional branch. This is an instruction which tells the computer to go to another part of the program if a certain statement is true. In the example on the right, line 60 sends the computer to a **subroutine** if Y is equal to I divided by X.

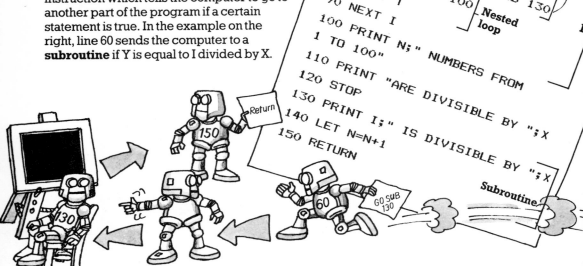

```
5 REM NUMBER DIVIDER PROGR
10 PRINT "GIVE ME A NUMBER"
20 INPUT X
30 LET N=0        Assignment
                  statement
40 FOR I=1 TO 100
50 LET Y=INT(I/X)   Conditional
60 IF Y=I/X         branch
70 FOR T=1 TO 100   THEN GOSUB 130
80 NEXT T          Nested
90 NEXT I          loop
100 PRINT N;" NUMBERS FROM
1 TO 100"
110 PRINT "ARE DIVISIBLE BY ";X
120 STOP
130 PRINT I;" IS DIVISIBLE BY ";X
140 LET N=N+1
150 RETURN
```

Return

150

130

60

GO SUB 130

Subroutine

Functions

A computer has built-in instructions telling it how to carry out certain tasks – mathematical ones such as adding, multiplying and finding square roots, as well as many others such as moving the **cursor** to a certain position on the screen or picking out a letter from a **string variable**. All these tasks are known as functions and you tell the computer to carry them out either by pressing a key (e.g. +, *, /) or by typing a **keyword** such as TAB or MID$ in BASIC.

Some computers allow you to make up, or define, your own functions. You can make up a mathematical function using the BASIC command DEF FN, and on some computers you are also able to program special **function keys** (see page 7), so that the computer will carry out a specific task, or function, every time you press them.

Other words

Random number. This is a number which is unpredictable, like numbers produced by throwing dice. A computer has a special program which makes it produce random numbers.

Routine or **module.** These are general terms used to describe any part of a program which carries out one particular task and is complete in itself.

Procedure. This is another word for a **subroutine**, a separate section within a program which carries out one specific task.

Print formatting. This means arranging text on a screen in a particular way. In BASIC, you use **keywords** such as TAB or PRINT AT to tell the computer where to print the next word.

Loop. This makes the computer repeat a series of instructions a certain number of times. In BASIC, this is done with the words FOR, TO and NEXT. The loop from line 40 to line 90 on the left makes the computer carry out lines 50 to 80 a hundred times.

Nested loop. This is a loop within a loop and it makes the computer carry out a series of instructions each time the outer loop is repeated. In the program on the left, the nested loop from lines 70 to 80 is a **delay loop**. There are no instructions to carry out, but it makes the computer pause a moment while it counts through all the values from 1 to 100 for the **variable** T.

Subroutine. This is a special section of a program which carries out an often-needed task. Each time the task is needed, an instruction sends the computer to the subroutine. At the end of the subroutine the computer returns to where it left off. The subroutine on the left begins at line 130 and the RETURN instruction in line 150 makes it go back to line 70.

$$Y = INT(I/X)$$

Loop

Menu. This is a list of different choices which some types of program can give you. You choose what you want to do and the computer then runs that part of the program. A **menu-driven** program uses lots of menus at stages throughout its operation.

GIGO

GIGO stands for "garbage in, garbage out" – you can't expect good results if you give the computer rubbish!

Edit. This is to change and improve a program by re-writing parts of it, correcting mistakes and generally making sure that the program is how you want it.

Merge. This is to join two programs together to make one program.

Operators. These are the various symbols which a computer understands, such as / (divide), = (equals), > (greater than) and $ (string – the sign used to indicate letter data).

Delimiter. This is also called a **separator**. It is a symbol used to separate two items of information. Some BASIC examples are the commas between items in a DATA statement and the semi-colons separating items in a PRINT statement.

String delimiter. The quotation marks which must be put around a **string variable** in BASIC are string delimiters.

To return a value. A computer produces an answer, known as returning a value, after it has carried out a mathematical calculation.

String handling. This refers to the various things which can be done with **string variables**, such as selecting letters from a string or joining two strings together to make one long one. This last is known as **concatenation**.

Default. This describes anything which a computer does as a matter of course unless you tell it to do otherwise. For example, the default screen colour is the colour which appears when a computer is first switched on.

Parameter. This is a term generally used to mean the value of a **variable** which is passed to a **subroutine** or the limit of a block of data.

Software

All programs used by a computer are known as **software**. Those programs which are already built into the computer's memory are called **resident software**. They include the **operating system** (the programs which control the working of the computer) and the **utility programs** (see below). Those which are loaded from elsewhere, e.g. from cassette or disk, or typed in at the keyboard, are **non-resident software**.

Firmware. This is also known as **solid-state software**. It refers to any programs permanently stored in **ROM chips**, either in a computer's memory or in **cartridges** which can be plugged into the computer. The programs are called firmware because they cannot be erased.

Utility programs. These are sometimes called **system software**. They are programs which enable a computer to carry out frequently needed tasks, such as transferring data to cassette or disk. Most of the important utility programs are already built into the computer.

Programmer's toolkit. This is a collection of **utility programs** stored on a cassette, cartridge or disk, which are designed to make programming easier. A toolkit can contain many different programs, such as a program for renumbering or deleting blocks of program lines.

Sort. This is a program for re-arranging data, e.g. arranging lists in alphabetic or numeric order. There are lots of different kinds of sort program, each using a different technique. Some examples are **bubble, selection** and **partition** sorts. A sort may be one of the **utility programs** in a computer.

Words describing programs

User-friendly. Also called **user-oriented**, this type of program is easy to use and understand.

Structured. This type of program is made up of individual self-contained sections, each of which performs one specific task. It is usually easy to read and understand.

User-defined. This type of program is written especially to cater for one person's requirements.

Interactive. An interactive program is one in which there is communication between user and computer. An adventure game is one example and most programs used as educational aids are also interactive.

Portable. If a program can be run easily on a number of different computers, then it is portable.

Elegant. This describes any program which is stylishly written and which attracts admiration. It may or may not be a good program in other respects!

36

*For more about **databases** see page 26.

Applications programs

These are programs which carry out tasks for the user, as opposed to programs which control the working of the computer (see operating system, page 17).

```
WILDLIFE DATABASE

THE PANDA
---------

Lives in SE China
Size: 1.3 m long
Weight: 160 kg
Lifespan: 15-30 years
Carnivore and Herbivore
Feeds during the day
```

```
This book was written using a word
processing program. The text was
typed into the computer and
displayed on the screen. It was
then altered and corrected and the
final text was printed out on paper
and sent to a typesetter.

Copies 2; Document name :Jargon
SAVE PRINT EDIT SEARCH REPLACE COPY
```

Database program. This refers to any program which allows you to work with a collection of data – either your own data which you want to be able to catalogue and update, or data already provided in a field which interests you.

Expert system. This is a database-type program which contains a large amount of specialized data, e.g. engineering, medical or legal information. A person using the program types in certain facts and the computer uses its store of information to make a decision in an area where the opinion of an expert, or professional, would normally be needed.

Wordprocessor program. This is a program which makes it possible to alter and re-organize large blocks of text on the screen – adding lines and correcting mistakes as necessary. It is very useful for anyone writing long pieces of text.

Spreadsheet program. This type of program is used a lot in financial planning. It allows you to set up a "sheet" of data inside a computer's memory. You can look at any part of the sheet on the screen and change the data as necessary. If you change anything the computer readjusts other related pieces of data. **VisiCalc** is an example of such a program.

```
HAUNTED HOUSE

YOUR LOCATION: A DUSTY CELLAR

THERE IS AN
OLD CHEST
HERE

YOU CAN MOVE: N,S OR E

WHAT NEXT?
```

Simulation program. This is a type of program which produces a "model" of a real-life situation, such as the **flight simulation** program above. This is a games program but flight simulation is also used to train pilots. Simulation is used by manufacturers and builders, to "test" products before they are made, or in business or economic planning. This might be to work out the most efficient set-up for a company or to predict the future state of the world's economy.

Adventure game. An adventure game is dependent on a large store of data. During the game, various choices are offered to the player, who must act out a "dangerous" make-believe adventure, avoiding pitfalls and solving puzzles. To succeed in the game, the player must get out safely, having collected as much "treasure" as possible in most cases.

Machine code terms

A **machine code program** is a program written either completely in **hex** or in **assembly language**.* Each instruction in a machine code program deals directly with the contents of **memory locations** or with the **registers** – the **CPU**'s own store for data it is working on. The set of machine code instructions that a computer understands is known as its **instruction set**, and each instruction sets off one operation inside the computer. Below there are explanations of some of the words used to describe these operations.

Load. To take a copy of a piece of data from the memory and put it in a register.

Store. To take a copy of the contents of a register and put it in the memory.

Transfer. To take a copy of the data in a register and put it in another register.

Compare. To make the computer compare two pieces of data. The next instruction will usually be a **branch**.

Jump. This makes the computer go directly to a certain **memory address** or go a certain number of memory places forward or back to find its next instruction.

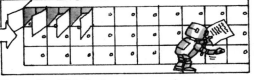

Branch. This is the same as a **jump**, except that the computer is always sent a certain number of places forward or back to find its next instruction.

Set. To make a particular **bit**, e.g. the **carry flag** (see page 16) equal to one.

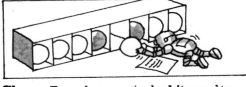

Clear. To make a particular **bit** equal to zero, or **reset** it.

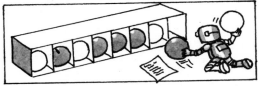

Increment. To add one to the contents of a register or memory location.

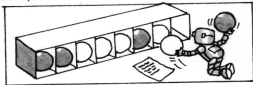

Decrement. To take one from the contents of a **register** or **memory location**.

*For more about **machine code, hex** and **assembly language**, see pages 30 and 31.

Addressing modes

Addressing modes are the different ways in which you can tell the computer where to find the next piece of data. Each machine code program line consists of two parts – the **operation code**, or **opcode**, which is the instruction, and the **operand** which tells the computer where to find the data to work on. Some of the most common addressing modes are listed below.

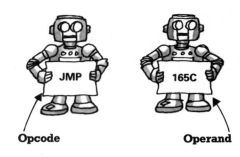

Opcode   Operand

Immediate addressing. In this mode the operand itself is the data. The opcode often contains the name of a register. This type of addressing is also called **explicit addressing**.

Direct or **absolute addressing.** The operand in this mode is the address where the data is to be found, known as the **direct** or **absolute address**.

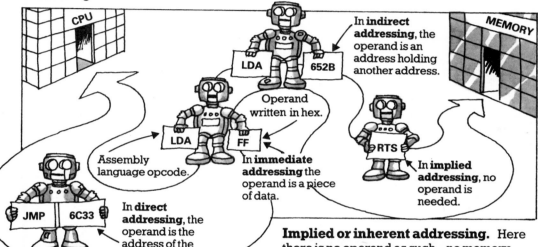

In **indirect addressing**, the operand is an address holding another address.

Operand written in hex.

Assembly language opcode.

In **immediate addressing** the operand is a piece of data.

In **implied addressing**, no operand is needed.

In **direct addressing**, the operand is the address of the data.

Indirect addressing. Here the operand is the address of a memory location or register where the address of the data is stored. The address given in the operand is known as the **action address, dispatch address** or **jump vector**.

Indexed addressing. In this mode, the operand is only part of the address needed. To complete it, the contents of a register called the **index register** must be added to it. The address stated by the operand is called the **base address**, the number in the index register is the **displacement value** or **offset** and the final address produced by adding the two together is the **effective address**. This mode is often used in conjunction with another mode – you can have **indirect indexed addressing**, for example.

Implied or inherent addressing. Here there is no operand as such – no memory address or register is stated and the computer knows what to do from the opcode itself.

Relative addressing. In this mode, the computer is told to look a certain number of memory places ahead or behind the one it is currently dealing with.

Zero page addressing. Here the operand is an address on the first **page** of the memory, called **page zero**. Each page of the memory usually contains 256 locations (see page 18), and zero page contains the first 256, numbered from 0 to 255. Most addresses take up two **bytes** of the memory but those on zero page can be held in one, i.e. they can be represented as a **binary** number of eight digits. In zero page addressing, therefore, only one byte is needed for the address and this makes it faster than other modes.

More machine code

A number of machine code instructions allow you to change the individual **bits** within a **byte**. Some of these instructions are for carrying out arithmetic, others are used for such things as moving **characters** across the screen. Below are explanations of some of the most common operations carried out by these instructions.

AND▶ In this operation, the computer compares the **binary code** for two pieces of data. It produces a 1 wherever there is a 1 in the same place in both bytes, otherwise it produces a 0.

◀OR. This operation produces a 1 if there is a 1 in either, or both of the two bytes.

XOR▶ Sometimes called **EOR**, this stands for exclusive OR. It produces a 1 if either, but not both, of the two bits is a 1.

◀NAND. This stands for **NOT AND** and it produces the **complement** (see **NOT**) of the number produced by **AND**ing two bytes.

NOT▲ This operation is often known as **flipping the bits** or **complementing**. It changes all the 1s in a byte to 0s, and all the 0s to 1s. The result of a NOT operation is called the **complement, one's complement** or **logical complement** of the original number. Added together, the original number and the complement will always produce 11111111 (decimal 255), and this fact is used as the basis of a number of mathematical operations.

NOR▶ This stands for **NOT OR**. It produces the **complement** (see **NOT**) of an **OR** result.

Shift. This operation "shifts" the bits of a byte one place to the left or the right. The bit which is "pushed" off the end is put in the **carry flag** (see page 16), and either a 1 or a 0 is put on at the other end, depending on the type of shift being used. There are several different types of shift which can be used for a number of different purposes. For example, a **shift right** can be used to halve a number, as in the example below. Here the **binary number** for 102 in decimal has become the binary version of 51. A **shift left** can be used in arithmetic to double a number. The example below shows how the binary version of 51 is doubled to 102.

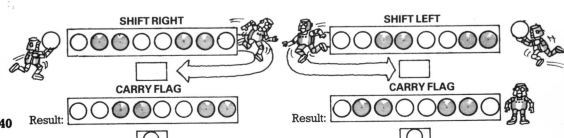

40 Result:

Rotate. This is like a **shift**, but the **bit** already in the **carry flag** (see page 16) is added to the other end of the byte.

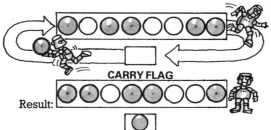

CARRY FLAG

Result:

Mask. If you want to look at one particular bit in a byte to see if it is a 1 or a 0, you make up a byte called a mask. This has seven 0s and one 1 – the 1 being in the same position as the bit you want to look at. If you carry out an **AND** operation on the mask and the byte to be tested, the result will either be 00000000 or the same as the mask.

For example, if you want to see if the third bit of a byte is a 1, you AND the byte with 00000100 (see below). If the third bit of the tested byte is a 1, you will get an answer of 00000100; if it is a 0, you will get 00000000. This is called **masking**.

To change the bit to 0, you AND the byte with the **complement** (see **NOT**) of the mask. If the bit was a 0, and you want to change it to a 1, you **OR** the byte with the mask (see below).

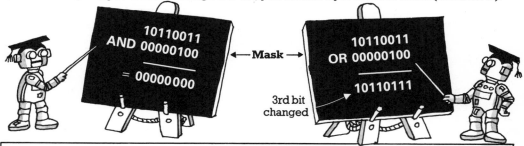

```
  10110011
AND 00000100
  = 00000000
```

← Mask →

```
  10110011
OR 00000100
  10110111
```

3rd bit changed

Negative numbers

Signed binary. This is one of the two main ways in which the **CPU** can handle negative numbers. It is not used in many computers nowadays, though, having been largely replaced by **two's complement notation** (see below). In signed binary, the leftmost bit of a byte is a **sign bit**, with a 0 for a negative number and a 1 for a positive one. Subtraction is carried out in exactly the same way as any subtraction, that is, with "borrowing".

Two's complement notation. This is the way that most computers handle negative numbers. The two's complement of a number is used as its negative equivalent and is formed by **complementing** (see **NOT**) the number and then adding 1. In fact, it is the **binary number** which, when added to the original number, produces 00000000 (with a 1 "carried up"). So the two's complement of 00110011 (decimal 51) for example, is 11001101. This is used to represent −51 in decimal.

In two's complement notation, the computer subtracts a number by adding its two's complement to the number it is to be subtracted from (see right). Effectively, this is the same as treating a decimal sum such as 106−51 as 106+(−51). If a sum produces a negative answer, e.g. 51−106, then this appears in two's complement form (see right).

106 →
−51 in two's complement →

```
  01101010
+ 11001101
= 00110111
```

55 →

−106 in two's complement →
51 →

```
  00110011
+ 10010110
= 11001001
```

−55 in two's complement →

41

Maths words and number systems

Argument. In a mathematical expression, such as SQR(9) (the BASIC command to find the square root of nine), the argument is the number that the function (see page 34) works on. In the example above, the square root function (SQR) is working on an argument of nine.

Exponent. This is a word for the power to which a number is raised. The exponent in the statement $X = 2^8$, for example, is 8.

Mantissa. Very large numbers are often written as a number times ten raised to a certain power. For example, 64×10^6 is 64 million. The number 64 is called the mantissa.

Boolean algebra

This is the system devised by George Boole, a 19th century Irish mathematician, which is the basis of computer logic. It is a set of rules based on the ability of statements to be true or false. Using these rules set out in **truth tables** such as the one on the right for operations such as **AND, OR** and **NOT** (see page 40), calculations based on logical ideas can be carried out. For example, the instruction IF A = 16 AND B = 20 THEN LET X = 10 would be carried out in this way:

AND			Truth table
1	AND	1	1
1	AND	0	0
0	AND	1	0
0	AND	0	0

In this table, a 1 indicates "true", and a 0 indicates "false".

Check A. If equal to 16, then "true".

Check B. If equal to 20, then "true".

1 AND 1 is 1.

Statement "true".

Make X equal to 10.

Number systems

Every number has its own **base number**, also called its **root** or **radix**. For example, our everyday decimal system has a base of ten. It uses ten digits (0-9), and in a number each digit is in a column whose value is ten times that of the one on its right, i.e. units, tens, hundreds, etc.

Binary. This uses only two digits, 0 and 1, and the value of each digit in a number is twice the one in the column on its right – units, twos, fours, eights, etc.

Octal. This uses eight digits, 0 to 7, and each digit in a number has a value which is eight times the one on its right – units, eights, sixty-fours, etc.

Hex. This is short for **hexadecimal**, a system which uses 16 digits, the numbers 0 to 9 and the letters A to F. The value of each hex column is 16 times the one on its right.

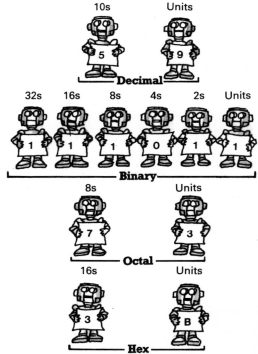

Decimal: 10s — 5, Units — 9

Binary: 32s — 1, 16s — 1, 8s — 1, 4s — 0, 2s — 1, Units — 1

Octal: 8s — 7, Units — 3

Hex: 16s — 3, Units — B

Computer sound

Many microcomputers have a **sound synthesizer** which can produce some form of music or sound. All sounds are produced by something vibrating in air and in a sound synthesizer the vibrations are made by a special electronic circuit called an **oscillator**. The more oscillators a computer has, the more sounds or notes it can produce at once (see **channel** below).

Waveform. The vibrations that produce a sound can be shown as a **wave**, made up of **cycles**. The shape of a wave is called the waveform and different sounds have different waveforms. For example, the same note played on a piano and a trumpet produces a different waveform and therefore sounds different.

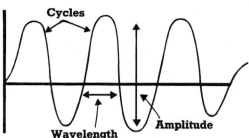

Wavelength. This is the distance between two points at the same place on two cycles of a wave.

Frequency. This is the measurement of the number of times one cycle is repeated in a second.

Amplitude. This is the volume or loudness of a note or sound.

Pitch. The pitch of a note is determined by its **frequency**. The greater the frequency, the higher the pitch.

Tone. A tone is a continuous sound or note produced by waves with a constant **frequency**.

White noise. This is the noise made by electrical interference. It is often used as an explosion sound in computer games programs.

Channel. A channel or **voice** on a computer produces one note or sound. In order to have more than one note playing at once, you need more than one channel.

Envelope. A note played by different instruments goes through different stages of volume and the term envelope refers to the pattern of volume variations created by one instrument. Some computers have **envelope generators** which enable them to reproduce the envelopes of different instruments.

The volume stages of a sound envelope are called **attack, decay, sustain** and **release**, often known as **ADSR**. The attack is the immediate rise in volume to its highest level when a note is first struck and the decay is the settling down of the note to a consistent level (the sustain level). The release is the falling away of the volume to zero at the end of the note.

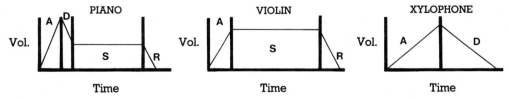

Speech synthesis. Also known as **voice output**, this is the process by which a computer can be programmed to produce sounds like human speech. The most common method of doing this involves the sounds of a vocabulary of words or syllables being stored in the computer's memory as electrical signals on certain **frequencies**. These are then produced when the word or group of syllables is typed on the keyboard.

Speech recognition. This is also known as **voice input**. It is more difficult to achieve than **speech synthesis**. It is the process of getting a computer to recognize spoken words by comparing them with stored patterns of electrical signals in its memory. The main difficulty is the fact that the same word spoken by two different people may sound different.

Wordfinder

This is a list of all the words which are defined in this book, as well as various symbols and number terms which come at the beginning. The page numbers written in **bold type** show the page where the main definition of a word appears.

45

First published in 1983 by Usborne Publishing Ltd, 20 Garrick Street, London WC2E 9BJ, England.
© 1983 Usborne Publishing.
The name Usborne and device ⚊ are Trade Marks of Usborne Publishing Ltd. All rights reserved.
No part of this publication may be reproduced, stored in a retrieval system or transmitted in any form
or by any means, electronic, mechanical, photocopying, recording or otherwise, without the prior
permission of the publisher.